JESUS
school of miracles

MINISTERING IN
SIGNS, WONDERS and MIRACLES

--- ❧ ---

Tom and Susie Scarrella

Jesus School of Miracles
ISBN 13: 978-0-9898828-1-1
ISBN 10: 0989882810
Copyright © 2013 Tom Scarrella

Published by
Tom Scarrella Ministries
P.O. Box 9427
Fort Lauderdale, FL. 33075

Visit our Website at
www.sharethefire.org

DEDICATION

We dedicate this book to our dearest, most loyal, honest, trustworthy, and selfless friends, Prophet Kobus and Annalise van Rensberg. We sincerely and humbly honor you both. Thank you for showing us the way to a true life of grace, sonship, and TRUTH — we are forever grateful. Prophet, we are the generation!

We would also like to dedicate this book to Pastor John Wimber. Your book, Power Evangelism changed my life and the course of my ministry over 20 years ago - it lit a flame within my heart for signs, wonders and lost souls, that will never go out. I am forever wrecked for anything less than a life of the powerful supernatural. Keep cheering us on from the great cloud of witnesses.

CONTENT

INTRODUCTION

Welcome to The *Jesus School of Miracles.* Can you imagine being trained for the ministry by the Master, Jesus, himself? Can you visualize yourself walking side-by-side with Him, like the disciples, traveling from the synagogue to the hillside, from the prayer meeting to the healing line, watching His every move, studying the way that He ministered to the people, learning how he confronted the religious, taking notes on how he cast out demons and healed the sick?

The life and ministry of Jesus is nothing short of amazing. On the big screen, Hollywood could never match the adventures of His three-year ministry. This life was filled with victories, contentions, power-encounters, rejection, temptations, and objections, as He was forever changing the culture, the religious beliefs, the people, and the world. Thankfully, much of His ministry was chronicled by those who knew Him best, by those who were found walking in His shadow down the dusty paths, by those who were there when he walked on the water and he fed the five thousand. These men were among those who watched the wonderful works performed by His hands. They witnessed the awesome freeing power that He functioned out of and there is no doubt that these men were touched by His fire, passion and the zeal for His Fathers business.

Remember back to when those W.W.J.D. bracelets became so popular? You remember, *What Would Jesus Do?* The intent of the bracelet was to provoke us to thought before action – to cause us to think about and consider what Jesus would do in our situation before we simply acted out our first impulses. They were trendy and fashionable and they were great, but there was one major problem with these bracelets. That problem was that most people didn't have a clue about what Jesus would do in most situations. Sure, they had their opinion about what He would do, and their opinion was usually based on a puddle-deep relationship that began and ended with Sunday school lessons as a kid or nursery rhymes. They defined what Jesus would do, not based on their experience or relationship with Him, but by what modern-day, watered-down religion or secular humanism had fed to them.

So, what would Jesus do? That's easy. He would heal the sick. He would cast out devils. He would raise the dead. He would set the oppressed free. He would heal the hurting. He would mend the broken. He would confront the religious. He would give mercy to the prostitute. He would cleanse the leper. He would welcome the outcast. He would speak to the storm. He would take the low seat. He would only speak the Truth. He would walk on water. He would 'hang-out' with sinners. He would defend the weak. He would curse the fig tree. He would die for the whole of humanity. *That* is what Jesus would do. Now, *what* will you do?

The *Jesus School of Miracles* is a training program that anyone can attend. You won't need to relocate or take a loan out to cover the tuition.

The *Jesus School of Miracles* is a clear, non-confusing, non-religious guide to the miraculous workings of Jesus Christ. Learning from His life and ministry, this school will stir-up your hunger for the things of God's Kingdom. It will equip you to function in the realm of miracles, signs and wonders more than ever before. And best of all, it will point your heart in the direction of the lost with a passionate purpose, just like Jesus.

Signs, Wonders and Miracles

"Therefore we must give the more earnest heed to the things we have heard, lest we drift away. For if the word spoken through angels proved steadfast, and every transgression and disobedience received a just reward, how shall we escape if we neglect so great a salvation, which at the first began to be spoken by the Lord, and was confirmed to us by those who heard Him, God also bearing witness both with signs and wonders, with various miracles, and gifts of the Holy Spirit, according to His own will?" (Hebrews 2:1-4 NKJV)

"But Peter, standing up with the eleven, raised his voice and said to them, "Men of Judea and all who dwell in Jerusalem, let this be known to you, and heed my words. For these are not drunk, as you suppose, since it is only the third hour of the day. But this is what was spoken by the prophet Joel: And it shall come to pass in the last days, says God, That I will pour out of My Spirit on all flesh; Your sons and your daughters shall prophesy, Your young men shall see visions, Your old men shall dream dreams. And on My menservants and on my maidservants I will pour out My Spirit in those days; and they shall prophesy. I will show wonders in heaven above, and signs in the earth beneath: Blood and fire and vapor of smoke. The sun shall be turned into darkness, and the moon into blood, before the coming of the great and awesome day of the LORD. And it shall come to pass that whoever calls on the name of the LORD Shall be saved.' "Men of Israel, hear these words: Jesus of Nazareth, a Man attested by God to you by miracles, wonders, and signs which God did through Him in your midst, as you yourselves also know." (Acts 2:14-22 NKJV)

THE DIVINE DANCE

All of God's promises, His presence, power, provision, and blessings are distributed to mankind on a conditional basis. Most principles of the Kingdom of God function in a pattern that we like to call, "a divine dance." Ask any young person planning for prom night whether it is possible or not to dance without the cooperation of their partner. It would be impossible. Dancing is much like our relationship to God. We cannot move without God moving with us, and God cannot move unless we, His partner move with Him. In Acts 2:17-21 God says, *"I will..."* followed by *"...you shall."* God initiates signs, wonders, and miracles, and mankind must reciprocate. Signs, wonders, and miracles are performed based upon the response and willingness of man. We are the vessel God has chosen to perform through.

According to Hebrew thought, it is believed that everything, both in heaven and in the earth, find its beginning and its end in a circular motion. For example, James 4:7 instructs, *"Draw near to God, and He will draw near to you,"* therefore mankind is beginning the circle by drawing near to God and God is completing the circle by drawing near to us – *The Divine Dance*.

- Signs, Wonders and Miracles always **touch the intellect** of man
- Signs, Wonders and Miracles always **touch the will** of man
- Signs, Wonders and Miracles always **touch the emotions** of man
- Signs, Wonders and Miracles are utilized to **capture the attention** of man
- Signs, Wonders and Miracles always **direct mankind toward God**
- Signs, Wonders and Miracles were the reason that God **"commended" Jesus' ministry**

SIGNS

Signs, or "supernatural tokens, omens, expressions, or supernatural origin," according to Greek translation, usually denote warnings.

WONDERS

Teras — Greek word for wonders, meaning "extraordinary occurrences." Note: Wonders are always plural.

Signs and Wonders are almost always mentioned together. Some great examples include: Jesus multiplying food, walking on water, fishing for coin in the mouth of the fish, people acting drunk in the upper room when God's Spirit filled them, falling to the ground under the power, speaking in the native tongues of others, speaking in other tongues, translation, dead saints appeared, etc.

We see many of those strange signs and wonders performed throughout church history and through to today. More examples include, gold dust appearing, levitation, joy of the Lord hit people and they laugh for hours, supernatural wind appears in a service, sparks coming from the hands of men and women, and even statutes came to life. These all have a tremendous effect of the fear of God upon man, both saved and unsaved!

MIRACLES

The Greek word for Miracles is, *"dunamis,"* meaning power or inherent ability.

Miracles, or "dunamis power," are used for works of a supernatural origin and character, which could not be produced by natural agents and means.

"The former account I made, O Theophilus, of all that Jesus began both to do and teach, until the day in which He was taken up, after He through the Holy Spirit had given commandments to the apostles whom He had chosen, to whom He also presented Himself alive after His suffering by

many infallible proofs, being seen by them during forty days and speaking of the things pertaining to the kingdom of God. And being assembled together with them, He commanded them not to depart from Jerusalem, but to wait for the Promise of the Father, "which," He said, "you have heard from Me; for John truly baptized with water, but you shall be baptized with the Holy Spirit not many days from now." Therefore, when they had come together, they asked Him, saying, "Lord, will you at this time restore the kingdom to Israel?" And He said to them, "It is not for you to know times or seasons which the Father has put in His own authority. But you shall receive power when the Holy Spirit has come upon you; and you shall be witnesses to Me in Jerusalem, and in all Judea and Samaria, and to the end of the earth." (Acts 1:1-8 NKJV)

DUNAMIS POWER
MIRACLE WORKING POWER

As stated earlier, the Greek word for Miracles is, dunamis, but notice that it is the same word for Power, therefore, it also could be said, "miracle working power." Acts 1:1-8 reveals a promise of POWER! In fact, Acts 1:8 is the key scripture of the New Testament.

In Acts 1:8, POWER is what we are promised, not speaking in tongues. Often believers are focused and have compromised on the ability to speak in other tongues, instead of being in pursuit of the power of God. We must realize that we are a people who have been endued with POWER from on high. When power was received in Acts 2, clearly the power is what became the Sign and Wonder for all the world to see.

EXAMPLES OF DUNAMIS POWER

Katherine Kuhlman, a great healing evangelist of the 1960s, would often times experience a physical wind blowing into her healing crusades. The wind was visibly on the people walking the isles. During her meetings the power of God would move so majestically that the sick would many times be healed before they approached the platform and often times while they waited in line to enter the building. Another incident of a sign and wonder that commonly occurred in her ministry would happen as she was escorted through the kitchen after the meetings and all the unsaved cooks and kitchen staff would fall to the ground under the power of God.

Signs, wonders, and miracles are often supernatural occurrences that happen to individuals when they experience a touch by the glory and power of God. There are numerous accounts of Signs, Wonders, and Miracles seen throughout the Gospels and in the book of Acts. Here are only a couple scriptural examples:

- The sick were healed as Peter's shadow fell upon them
- Demons cast out of individuals as Paul's handkerchief was laid upon them
- Individuals would fall into trances
- To pay taxes Peter went fishing and found money in the mouth of the fish
- More than five-thousand people were fed from a single boys meal with twelve full baskets left-over

Once while ministering in the state of Minnesota a young eight year-old girl attended the meeting with her parents. I called her forward in order to pray for her. As we prayed she went into a trance for an entire eight hour period. She stood there in front of the building speaking in tongues the entire eight hours, but didn't move a muscle. She later explained how she had walked with Jesus in heaven during that time. I experienced another incident while I was ministering in California when we laid hands on a woman who froze into a trance, unable to move, for several hours by the power of God.

These strange occurrences of supernatural, dunamis, power are what brought validation to the ministry of Jesus on earth. They are what validate the message of God's Kingdom in every ministry. Why then has the modern day church allowed itself to remain in a dormant, powerless state of function for so long? Being dormant does nothing except keep believers untouched by the power of the living God; it is shameful and pharisaic. It's time for the sons of God to recognize who they are and what they have inherited and arise by expecting these supernatural occurrences in our churches and ministries in order that our message may be valid before God in and win the world to Him.

Healing is Always the Will of God

*"When He had come down from the mountain, great multitudes followed Him. And behold, a leper came and worshiped Him, saying, "Lord, if You are willing, You can make me clean." Then Jesus put out His hand and touched him, saying, "**I am willing**; be cleansed." Immediately his leprosy was cleansed."* (Matthew 8:1-3 NKJV)

There are many doctrinal opinions running rampant within the modern day church. One common doctrinal pillar that most can agree upon is that of man's need for initial salvation from sin and death. Jesus died for the forgiveness of sin and He died so that the wall of separation between God and man would be brought down. Most "Christian" schools of thought do not have a problem with either of these issues when it comes to Jesus' work on the cross. The argument usually begins with the finished work of Jesus on Calvary's cross in relation to His being bruised and beaten for our healing.

God is not confused. God's Word is clear on His will for mankind in regard to healing. Notice that His Word doesn't say, "I am the Lord that makes you sick to teach you something," yet such foolish preaching comes from many pulpits today.

The very first and most important principle that must be settled in your heart, whether in ministering healing or receiving healing, is that it is **ALWAYS** God's will to heal everyone all the time. People that have not settled this issue will never see a flow of miracles or healing in their midst.

While some Christian groups believe that healing was not paid for through Jesus' death on the cross, another group argues that it is

God's will to heal only on occasion, but on other occasions He may will not to heal. This double-minded way of thinking is not biblical. Think of it this way, would you say to someone, "God sometimes forgives sin, but other times, as sovereign as God is, He chooses not to forgive. After all, He is God!" Of course you wouldn't. By using that analogy you can begin to see the heresy behind this thinking. The Scripture is clear - Isaiah 53:5 unequivocally states, *"But He was wounded for our transgressions, He was bruised for our iniquities; the chastisement for our peace was upon Him, and by His stripes we are healed."*

HEALING ONLY THROUGH FAITH

If the issue that Jesus always wants to heal you and heal others through you hasn't been settled in your heart then you will continually find yourself ministering or being ministered to only in the realm of "hope." Hope is a scriptural principle; however the difference between hope and faith is that hope doesn't heal. In the Word of God people aren't healed by their hope, they are healed only by their FAITH.

It is continually written throughout the Scriptures, *"Jesus said, your FAITH has healed you..."* The difference between hope and faith is that faith says *"now,"* while hope says *"not today, but hold on until another day."* Jesus and His disciples preached, ministered, and lived a "now" life, not a "one day soon" life. Examine their lives and their ministries. They existed both as though today was their last day on earth, as well as if they were the immortal generation that would not see death. Their faith in God's healing power for today was settled in their heart and as a result, they brought deliverance and salvation NOW to those who were dying and hurting, instead of just hoping for it one day to come.

DEVELOPING FAITH

A large portion of healing in the New Testament shows that FAITH is vital to receive, whether that faith comes by the recipient or by the minister. There also must be a development of faith in God's ability to confirm His Word. Faith is gained where the will of

God is known. If the will of God is unknown then it becomes impossible to exercise faith. Moreover, if a believer is unclear about the will of God on a specific subject, such as healing, then the believer also is unclear about the Word of God on that subject. The Bible tells us, *"Faith comes by hearing and hearing the Word of God."* Two ways to develop faith in God's ability to confirm His Word is by reading the Word of God and practicing the Word of God. Reading the Word of God isn't enough. In fact, reading the Word of God and not doing the Word of God will lead only to spiritual frustration. By choosing to do the Word in daily life you will begin to see the faithful hand of Jesus extended to heal the sick through you.

"... who Himself bore our sins in His own body on the tree, that we, having died to sins, might live for righteousness - by whose stripes you **were** *healed."* (1 Peter 2:24 NKJV)

WE WERE vs. WE ARE

In I Peter 2:24, Peter quotes the book of Isaiah in part as he is under the influence of the Holy Spirit. Notice that Peter is pictorially looking back to the cross using the words, *"we were healed..."* while Isaiah is looking forward to the cross using the words *"we are healed..."* Like Peter, we too are looking back to an event that is in the past. That past event caused our sins to be forgiven and our sicknesses to be healed. By looking back at the cross we see that healing is not our idea, but it originated with God and brought to us through the death of His son, Jesus.

Many Christian denominations foolishly believe that healing is man's idea and that man must try to manipulate God to do something that He really doesn't want to do. The truth is that God Himself initiated healing. It wasn't man, it was God who said, *"by His stripes we were healed"* and *"they shall lay hands on the sick and they shall be healed."*

A basic element of biblical interpretation is that when God sets a precedent or a pattern on a certain subject He rarely changes. In the Old Testament God told the people of Israel, *"I am the Lord that heals you...*" God set a precedent. The God of the Old Testament was a healer (Jehovah Rapha) and He is the God who changes not. So then, if God's Word is true, how could those of the Old Testament have healing, but it has ceased for today?

The ABC's of Faith

"Now faith is the substance of things hoped for, the evidence of things not seen." (Hebrews 11:1 NKJV)

"So then faith comes by hearing, and hearing by the word of God." (Romans 10:17 NKJV)

THE ABC'S OF FAITH

- What faith is
- How faith comes
- How faith is released

WHAT IS FAITH?

Faith is a persuasion, a conviction based upon what you have heard.

We must have faith that God can heal and that God is willing to heal. Again, faith is a persuasion, a conviction based upon what we have heard. Some believe that sickness and disease are given to man from God in order to teach us something. That belief is wicked – for it is wicked to call good, evil and to call evil, good. James 1:17, *"Every good and perfect gift is from above, coming down from the Father of the heavenly lights, who does not change like shifting shadows."* Is sickness and disease a good and perfect thing? The very word disease means DIS-EASE, illustrating a lack of ease in the body. God is good. He only gives good and perfect things. Set your doctrine right and then walk in faith.

If sickness and disease are the will of God for an individual then it would be against the will of God for that individual to visit his or her doctor. By believing that sickness and disease come from God in order to teach us something then seeking help from a doctor would place us out of the will of God. The lack of logic and truth is obvious; it is senseless religion, which produces no good or lasting fruit. Faith reaches into tomorrow and pulls into today what is needed, such as salvation, healing, and deliverance, along with every other good and perfect thing. Faith is a persuasion, a conviction, and "warranty deed" to our salvation, healing, deliverance, prosperity, provision, and surplus.

HOW FAITH COMES

Faith comes by hearing and hearing by the Word of God.

The way faith comes is easy. In fact, it would be difficult to argue another method of receiving faith because Scripture is so very clear. Romans 10:17 affirms that faith comes by hearing and hearing by the Word of God. Hebrews 11:1 reveals the timeline of faith. *"Now faith is..."* Faith is always for now. If an individual chooses not to bring God's promise of salvation into the timeline of now, then they may die and go to Hell knowing that Jesus already paid the price for their sin but not having simply acted on that knowledge. And the same is true for healing and deliverance.

HOW FAITH IS RELEASED

Faith is released by words and/or actions.

The manner in which faith is released can be found in the story of the woman with the issue of blood, as well as in the story of Jairus and his daughter, both found in Mark 5. In these two stories, we find that they released their faith by using both words and actions. James says, *"Faith without works is dead being alone."* Faith must be released by actions. The reason people struggle with their faith level is that they don't understand that they are required to do something with that faith. Heaven is already in motion on behalf of the person, but if he/she remains unmotivated or unmovable, it renders the promises of God useless and makes them of no effect in their life. In His ministry, Jesus always gave a faith command to the sick. For example he said to the lame man, *"take up your bed and walk,"* or *"arise and be healed."* To the blind eyes He commanded, *"be opened."* To the man with the withered hand He commanded, *"Stretch forth your hand."* Jesus showed to us that action is the main requirement to activate faith.

The Integrity of God's Word

"For the word of God is living and powerful, and sharper than any two-edged sword, piercing even to the division of soul and spirit, and of joints and marrow, and is a discerner of the thoughts and intents of the heart." (Hebrews 4:12-13 NKJV)

"(as it is written, "I have made you a father of many nations") in the presence of Him whom he believed - God, who gives life to the dead and calls those things which do not exist as though they did; who, contrary to hope, in hope believed, so that he became the father of many nations, according to what was spoken, "So shall your descendants be." And not being weak in faith, he did not consider his own body, already dead (since he was about a hundred years old), and the deadness of Sarah's womb. He did not waver at the promise of God through unbelief, but was strengthened in faith, giving glory to God, and being fully convinced that what He had promised He was also able to perform. And therefore "it was accounted to him for righteousness." Now it was not written for his sake alone that it was imputed to him..." (Romans 4:17-23 NKJV)

The core of the power of faith is integrity (truth, honor, veracity) on God's Word. God's Word is good and God will not allow one word to fail to come to pass. God is a God of integrity. He has always been and will always continue to be. His promises are YES and AMEN. His promises and His judgments are final and His Word is truth to all.

In all our years of ministerial experience we have learned that some Christians would much prefer to hear us preach a "no fault religion." When they hear a faith message they find it harsh, conditional, or insensitive. They would like God to maintain His integrity while they require and uphold none from themselves. However, to have faith is to be responsible with God's Word and with His Kingdom. As students in The Jesus School of Miracles we must develop an appetite for discipline and responsibility to our faith.

As discussed earlier, faith is a persuasion or a confidence. Hebrews 10 says not to cast away your confidence that has great reward. Humility, or having a humble spirit, isn't the same as being "run over" by the devil. Being humble involves walking in authority as a son of God, a brother of Christ. Faith demands boldness, and having a courageous confidence in God and in what He has already done on the cross.

RECEIVE HEALING FOR YOURSELF

When a believer finds themselves in the midst of struggle with sickness or disease they are often confronted with many questions, as well as feeling fearful and discouraged. When we experience this for ourselves or with others we must frequently remind ourselves that we are the sons of God and that "healing is the children's bread" as Matthew 15 instructs. Our heavenly Father has provided healing for us through our Lord Jesus. That healing is ours, if only we believe.

Jesus said, *"Do not fear, and only believe."* (Mark 5:36; Luke 8:50)

"And often he has thrown him both into the fire and into the water to destroy him. But if You can do anything, have compassion on us and help us." Jesus said to him, 'If you can believe, all things are possible to him who believes." (Mark 9:22-23 NKJV)

While conversing with Jesus, this man says, *"...If YOU can do anything, help us."* Pay attention to how Jesus replies. Jesus confronted this man's unbelief with correction and said, *"If YOU can believe ...*" The healing of this man's son was not solely dependent upon Jesus, but rather, his healing depended upon what he would or would not believe.

The pleading unbelief of this father is the same message that rings out in churches every Sunday. They believe in a healing Jesus, yet teach, "to you God says yes, to another God says no, and yet to another He says wait a while." Although this type of teaching may sound good, doesn't offend religion, and makes people feel good, it's completely unscriptural. Most often believers do not have a problem with believing that their sins were forgiven at conversion, but for some reason they change the biblical interpretation when it comes to receiving or administering healing. The Bible is extremely clear, healing is never based on God's ability, but it is based on man's willingness to believe. God has the ability to heal, deliver, or to rocket someone to the planet Mars by noon. The issue is not with God's ability, but man's willingness to believe. Jesus didn't say, "according to MY faith be it unto you." No. He said, *"according to YOUR faith be it unto you."*

When we are in need of healing or miracles, of any kind, there are three things that we must always do:

- Read the Word of God constantly
- Engage in as many worship services as possible
- Pray in tongues continually

> *"My son, give attention to my words; Incline your ear to my sayings. Do not let them depart from your eyes; Keep them in the midst of your heart; For they are life to those who find them, And health to all their flesh. Keep your heart with all diligence, For out of it spring the issues of life. Put away from you a deceitful mouth, And put perverse lips far from you."* (Proverbs 4:20-24 NKJV)

Be encouraged. Healing belongs to you now. You are not waiting on God, but rather it is He that is waiting on you!

"...how God anointed Jesus of Nazareth with the Holy Spirit and with power, who went about doing good and healing all who were oppressed by the devil, for God was with Him. And we are witnesses of all things, which He did..." (Acts 10:38-39 NKJV)

Healing Thoughts

"...how God anointed Jesus of Nazareth with the Holy Spirit and with power, who went about doing GOOD and healing all who were oppressed by the devil, for God was with Him. And we are witnesses of all things, which He did..." (Acts 10:38-39 NKJV)

HEALING IS GOOD

Luke, the author of the New Testament book of Acts, unquestionably tells us that healing is good. *"Jesus of Nazareth with the Holy Spirit and with power, who went about doing GOOD and healing all."* Knowing this, how is it possible for some to believe that healing is bad and that sickness is at times given to us by God and that ultimately sickness is "normal" for man to experience?

"My son, give attention to my words; Incline your ear to my sayings. Do not let them depart from your eyes; Keep them in the midst of your heart; For they are life to those who find them, And health to all their flesh. Keep your heart with all diligence, For out of it spring the issues of life. Put away from you a deceitful mouth, And put perverse lips far from you." (Proverbs 4:20-24 NKJV)

Proverbs 4:20-24 says His Word is life to those who find it, and health and healing to their flesh. Notice that it doesn't say that His Word is death and sickness to their bodies. FF Bosworth, a famous healing evangelist and writer, wrote in his book *Christ the Healer*,

"When your eyes are upon your symptoms and your mind is occupied with them more that with God's word, you have in the ground the wrong kind of seed for the harvest that you

desire. You have in the ground seeds of doubt. You are trying to raise one kind of a crop from another kind of seed. It is impossible to sow tares and reap wheat. Your symptoms may point to death, but God's word points you to life, and you cannot look in the opposite directions at the same time."

On the topic of disease FF Bosworth writes, *"It is impossible to boldly claim by faith a blessing which we are not sure God offers, because the power of God can be claimed only where the will of God is known."* In other words, we need to boldly claim by faith the blessings of God, but if we are unsure of God's will on a subject then it is difficult, and sometimes impossible to have faith for what we need.

"...while we do not look at the things which are seen, but at the things which are not seen. For the things which are seen are temporary, but the things which are not seen are eternal." (II Corinthians 4:18 NKJV)

WHY SOME ARE NOT HEALED

- Insufficient instruction
- Ignorance of the will of God. Jesus showed us that He wanted healing done publicly so that all would know that God's will is to heal
- Community of unbelief (Mark 6:5-6)
- The traditions of men
- Unbelief of the person ministering healing
- It is the work of an evil spirit in that person's body and needs to be cast out
- Non-forgiveness, spiritually lukewarm, or sin
- No expectancy for healing to occur
- No action of faith on the person receiving prayer

HEALING MISCONCEPTIONS

Many misconceptions haunt the Church today when it comes to faith healing. Let us discuss some of the most prevalent:

1. **Healing Passed Away with the Apostles**
    Many believers suppose that healing belonged to a dispensation, which passed away with the death of the apostles. Because of the lack of God's power in their life, they look for reasons or excuses as to why they are not healed. Ironic enough, these same ones are quick to follow the regimen of prescribed medication from their physician. It is hypocritical to say that God allows sickness or disease and that healing has passed away, and then advise a physician. Would they not then be trying to get out of the will of God by taking medicine and seeing a doctor?

2. **God Will Heal Just Because There is a Need for Healing**
    I challenge you to find anywhere in the Bible that God heals simply because there is a need to heal. Good luck. God is not moved by need. He is only moved by our faith. If it were true then one would be hard pressed to find anyone or anything who is suffering with any sickness or disease. If God were reacted based only on a need then countries like Ethiopia and India, who are stricken with poverty and disease, would be among the wealthiest and healthiest nations on Earth. An individual's need only moves people and faith is the only element that moves the hand of God.

3. **Throwing Away Prescription Eyeglasses Proves Faith**
    During our lifetime of ministry we have heard many ridiculous things and this misconception ranks among the worst. We have encountered those who have dumped their medicine down the drain and claimed it to be a step of faith. Don't be fooled, this is not faith at all. Receiving a healing has nothing to do with what one is NOT confessing or NOT doing, but what an individual IS confessing or IS doing.

PAUL'S THORN IN THE SIDE

"It is doubtless not profitable for me to boast. I will come to visions and revelations of the Lord: I know a man in Christ who fourteen years ago -- whether in the body I do not know, or whether out of the body I do not know, God knows -- such

*a one was caught up to the third heaven. And I know such a man -- whether in the body or out of the body I do not know, God knows -- how he was caught up into Paradise and heard inexpressible words, which it is not lawful for a man to utter. Of such a one I will boast; yet of myself I will not boast, except in my infirmities. For though I might desire to boast, I will not be a fool; for I will speak the truth. But I refrain, lest anyone should think of me above what he sees me to be or hears from me. And lest I should be exalted above measure by the abundance of the revelations, a **thorn in the flesh** was given to me, **a messenger of satan** to **buffet** me, lest I be exalted above measure. Concerning this thing I pleaded with the Lord three times that it might depart from me. And He said to me, "My grace is sufficient for you, for My strength is made perfect in weakness." Therefore most gladly I will rather boast in my infirmities, that the power of Christ may rest upon me. Therefore I take pleasure in infirmities, in reproaches, in needs, in persecutions, in distresses, for Christ's sake. For when I am weak, then I am strong."* (II Corinthians 12:1-10 NKJV)

It is obvious that Paul is referring and speaking of himself in this passage. This topic has become a point of major controversy for some circles of Christianity. Some actually believe that the thorn was an abscessed eye or another sickness of some sort. Others believe that Paul prayed and asked God to heal him and God answered and said "no."

Instead of reading into some secret meaning behind this in order to back up the denominations theological reasoning that sickness is given to us from God, let's set aside our presuppositions and religious, man-made teachings and read it with simplicity. The word "buffet" means "to suffer blow after blow." If it were pertaining to a sickness, it would then mean that Paul received a healing and then became stricken with sickness again and again, then receive healing and then again became sick.

To shed further light on the darkness of this belief ask yourself, who was the messenger that brought this "gift" of sickness? Would not all Christians agree that satan is responsible for bringing sickness, disease, and bondage? Do satan and God then work together?

> *"Do not be unequally yoked together with unbelievers. For what fellowship has righteousness with lawlessness? And what communion has light with darkness? And what accord has Christ with Belial? Or what part has a believer with an unbeliever?"* (II Corinthians 6:14-15 NKJV)

This teaching promotes satan to be the teacher of the church instead of the Holy Spirit. To say that a work of satan is our teacher is heresy.

The truth behind Paul's thorn is found in the book of Acts, which teaches that the thorn was **constant persecution from the religious** leaders of his day.

> *"But the Lord said to him, 'Go, for he is a chosen vessel of Mine to bear My name before Gentiles, kings, and the children of Israel. For I will show him how many things he must suffer for My name's sake.'"* (Acts 9:15-16)

> *"Therefore take careful heed to yourselves, that you love the Lord your God. Or else, if indeed you do go back, and cling to the remnant of these nations—these that remain among you—and make marriages with them, and go in to them and they to you, know for certain that the Lord your God will no longer drive out these nations from before you. But they shall be snares and traps to you, and scourges on your sides and thorns in your eyes, until you perish from this good land which the Lord your God has given you."* (Joshua 23:11-13)

In Acts 9:15-16, Jesus said from the beginning of Paul's ministry calling what the thorn was to be and from whom it would come. Joshua 23:11-13 contains a reference to *"thorns in the flesh,"* being the enemies of God who would bring persecution.

"Therefore most gladly I will rather boast in my infirmities, that the power of Christ may rest upon me. Therefore I take pleasure in infirmities, in reproaches, in needs, in persecutions, in distresses, for Christ's sake. For when I am weak, then I am strong." (II Corinthians 12:1-10 NKJV)

And lastly, in II Corinthians 12:10, Paul reveals exactly what the thorn was, *"infirmities, reproaches, needs, persecutions, distresses."* Paul later wrote that this thorn happened in his life after he had seen great and amazing things in the spiritual realm, which were so great that they were unlawful to speak. In other words, when he spoke of these amazing things the religious Jews denounced and persecuted him for speaking so boldly of our authority in Christ Jesus and our sonship in God our Father. Remember that Jesus too was persecuted for speaking of His Sonship.

*"And as His custom was, He went into the synagogue on the Sabbath day, and stood up to read. And He was handed the book of the prophet Isaiah. And when He had opened the book, He found the place where it was written: "The Spirit of the Lord is upon **ME**, Because He has anointed **ME** to preach the gospel to the poor; He has sent **ME** to heal the broken hearted, to proclaim liberty to the captives and recovery of sight to the blind, to set at liberty those who are oppressed; To proclaim the acceptable year of the Lord."... And He began to say to them, "**Today this Scripture is fulfilled in your hearing**."... So all those in the synagogue, when they heard these things, were filled with wrath, and rose up and thrust Him out of the city; and they led Him to the brow of the hill on which their city was built, that they might throw Him down over the cliff. Then passing through the midst of them, He went His way."* (Luke 4:16-28)

The religious Jews in the synagogue were filled with wrath and rose up to thrust Him out of their city and over the cliff. Jesus too had a thorn in his flesh — they were the religious Jews that wanted to kill Him. It was their unbelief that blinded them to who was in their very presence.

TROPIMUS I HAVE LEFT SICK

Another portion of Scripture that has left some believers in a theological melt down is in II Timothy 4. This scripture, and others, have been used to support a Calvinistic doctrine, which teaches that salvation is provided for some, but not for all.

"Erastus stayed in Corinth, but Trophimus I have left in Miletus sick." (II Timothy 4:20 NKJV)

Paul left behind Trophimus who was sick and/or unsaved. Some have argued that it was the will of God that he not be healed or saved. This passage doesn't at all indicate that it was the will of God that he not be saved or that he remain sick. This scripture was simply speaking of the condition that Paul had last seen Trophimus.

WHAT ABOUT JOB?

"For the thing I greatly feared has come upon me, and what I dreaded has happened to me." (Job 3:25 NKJV)

This Scripture is the key verse in why devastation happened in the life of Job. Job discloses that he was at fault by "opening the door" of fear. In fact, God later speaks to Job asking him, *"where were you..."* and the Bible makes known that Job then repented.

When we read scriptures it is important that we interpret its meaning through the eyes of Jesus. Some will look to Job and his situation to be our pattern, but as New Testament Christians, Jesus is our example. When we read scriptures it is also important that we interpret its meaning after we have read the scripture in its entire context and with the entire content. Later in the book of Job we learn that Job received healing and that he prospered beyond that of what he had nine months previous, and he did this because he opened the door of blessing through repentance. This story of Job illustrates for us the possibility that through our belief or unbelief and fear we open our lives to cursing, as well as to God's blessing. It further illustrates the overwhelming goodness, grace and mercy of our Father.

Methods of Ministering and Receiving Healing

The scriptures provide many methods of administering healing and many methods of receiving healing. These methods include:

- *Laying on of hands*
- *Prayer of faith*
- *Anointing oil*
- *Blessed cloths*

Following are two methods most frequently used throughout the New Testament.

- *Laying on of hands*
- *Prayer of faith (spoken word)*

LAYING ON OF HANDS

The laying on of hands is a placing of natural hands upon a natural sickness/disease bringing about a miracle or healing. Laying on of hands was an **elementary** principle of the first church found in Hebrews 6. And it remains a common method of how individuals are filled with the Holy Ghost, healed, and set free.

*"Therefore, leaving the discussion of the elementary principles of Christ, let us go on to perfection, not laying again the foundation of repentance from dead works and of faith toward God, of the doctrine of baptisms, of **laying on of***

hands, of resurrection of the dead, and of eternal judgment..." (Hebrews 6:1-3)

*"And He said to them, "Go into all the world and preach the gospel to every creature. He who believes and is baptized will be saved; but he who does not believe will be condemned. And these signs will follow those who believe: In My name they will cast out demons; they will speak with new tongues; they will take up serpents; and if they drink anything deadly, it will by no means hurt them; they [the believing ones] shall **lay hands on the sick**, and they will recover."* (Mark 16:15-18 NKJV)

Naturally speaking, the result of laying on of hands makes no logical sense. But the natural mind often forgets the "super" element that God's anointing brings to the natural realm, therefore creating a supernatural kingdom. The two main methods of healing used in the life and ministry of Jesus was the laying on of hands the method of the spoken Word.

"The Law of Contact and Transmission will bring healing to the sick. When a person lays hands on the sick in obedience to this spiritual law, then the contact of those hands will transmit God's healing power to the sick. The believer also has to exercise faith for the law to work."
- Kenneth Hagin

Our faith attracts the power of God and it activates the power of God in our lives and in the lives of those to whom we minister. As a minister of healing, it is our part of faith that will ignite the activity of God's power to flow from us into the body of those who are afflicted with sickness, pain, etc. By laying our hands, in faith, on another person we are actually transferring the power or anointing of God into their very being. We are working our faith and they are receiving from God through us.

Regrettably, the laying on of hands is one of the most abused aspects of many ministries. Pushing or forcing people to fall down, messing-up their hair, and touching people inappropriately are all examples of excess and abuse in this area. While the scriptures are not practically clear on how the laying on of hands should be dispensed, the scripture is clear on the appropriate spirit in which it should be carried out — a humble, gentle, meek, and boldly confident spirit.

SCRIPTURAL "HOW TO"

The biblical "How To" in laying on of hands can be seen over and over again throughout the ministries of Jesus and His disciples, as well as others who ministered to the sick. By their example, we learn that they didn't PRAY for the sick, rather they HEALED the sick. They laid their hands upon the sick or they simply spoke the Word of life. Take note also of the amount of instructions given to the person receiving the ministry, prior to the laying on of hands. Many well established and experienced ministers will admit a direct correlation between properly instructing those with whom are receiving the ministry and them actually receiving their healing. Instead of carelessly or quickly "slapping hands" on the sick and hoping for something to happen, set them up to receive their healing by instructing them in faith with simplicity (what faith is, where faith comes, and how faith works).

PRAYER OF FAITH

The prayer of faith is just that, a PRAYER of faith. It is obviously prayer that involves faith. Faith is a confident knowing that a thing will come to pass before it is actually manifested. The prayer of faith is the number one way to **receive** healing, breakthrough, etc. from God.

Faith must first be built into the mind of an individual prior to receiving healing, therefore once an individual hears that it is God's will for them to be healed, that God can and will heal them; they are ready to receive their healing.

*"And **the prayer of faith** will save the sick, and the Lord will raise him up. And if he has committed sins, he will be forgiven."* (James 5:15-16 NKJV)

*"So Jesus answered and said to them, **"Have faith in God**. For assuredly, I say to you, whoever says to this mountain, 'Be removed and be cast into the sea,' and does not doubt in his heart, but believes that those things he says will be done, he will have whatever he says. Therefore I say to you, whatever things you ask when you pray, believe that you receive them, and you will have them."* (Mark 11:22-24 NKJV)

Mark 11:23-24 saying; *"say to this mountain,"* *"believes what he says,"* and *"he will have whatever he says."* Do you see the instructions?

Mark continues, *"Whatever THINGS you ask for..."* God is asking you what your desired end result will be beforehand. What is it that you would like to see made manifested? It is important for the minister who is praying to visualize, by learning to speak, what they desire to have or see after they have prayed and asked. This will result in the miraculous. Realize that God has no problem with getting us those THINGS when we have faith and belief to spiritually see it manifested before it is actually made manifest into reality, and then speak (instruct) its full manifestation.

ANOINTING WITH OIL

*"Is anyone among you suffering? Let him pray. Is anyone cheerful? Let him sing psalms. Is anyone among you sick? **Let him call for the elders** of the church, and **let them pray** over him, **anoiting him <u>with oil</u>** in the name of the Lord. And the prayer of faith will save the sick, and the Lord will raise him up. And if he has committed sins, he will be forgiven. Confess your trespasses to one another, and pray for one another, that you may be healed. The effective, fervent prayer of a righteous man avails much. Elijah was a*

man with a nature like ours, and he prayed earnestly that it would not rain; and it did not rain on the land for three years and six months. And he prayed again, and the heaven gave rain, and the earth produced its fruit. Brethren, if anyone among you wanders from the truth, and someone turns him back, let him know that he who turns a sinner from the error of his way will save a soul from death and cover a multitude of sins." (James 5:13-20 NKJV)

James, one of the disciples of Jesus, gave us a pattern to follow. He provides another method for what should be done prior to prayer, during prayer, and after prayer for the sick. Mark 6:13 reveals that Jesus' disciples administered healing to the sick using this method on occasion.

*"And they cast out many demons, and **anointed with oil** many who were sick, and healed them."* (Mark 6:13)

The question that James asks is very interesting, *"Is ANY sick among you?"* giving the impression that healing wasn't needed as much in the early church as in modern day. Healing was most needed among the unsaved and God was merciful to heal all. In most churches today the vast majority of its members are inflicted with sickness, disease, oppression, or torment, and yet many church leaders refuse to preach on healing and on God's divine power to heal.

Thankfully, as believers, we are not limited by our church leaders. We are each called and chosen to minister to the sick all the time. Healing the sick or ministering to the sick doesn't require a degree, a pulpit, or even ordination papers. It only requires a willing vessel full of confident faith in the finished work of the cross of Christ and a very willing and powerful God.

"And behold, a woman in the city who was a sinner, when she knew that Jesus sat at the table in the Pharisee's house, brought an alabaster flask of fragrant oil, and stood at His feet behind Him weeping; and she began to wash His feet with her tears, and wiped them with the hair of her head; and

she kissed His feet and anointed them with the fragrant oil." (Luke 7:37-38 NKJV)

"And they cast out many demons, and anointed with oil many who were sick, and healed them." (Mark 6:13 NKJV)

BLESSED CLOTHS

*"God did extraordinary miracles through Paul, so that even **handkerchiefs and aprons that had touched him were taken to the sick**, and their illnesses were cured and the evil spirits left them."* (Acts 19:11-12 NIV)

The blessing of cloths is the least seen method of healing throughout New Testament scripture. In Acts 19:11-12, Paul blesses handkerchiefs, aprons, or cloths of some sort, to bring healing to the sick. This was known to have happened if the sick individual was too far away. Much like the laying on of hands, this method is a transferring of power or anointing and the cloth acts as a "delivery tool" for the power and anointing. We like to refer to the blessed cloth as a point of contact. Like the laying on of hand, it also requires faith and the very method itself is faith in action. As uncommon as it may be in the scriptures, it is a very valid and effective method of ministering to the sick.

The extraordinary miracle of blessed cloths is not the same as "standing in proxy." The method of "standing in proxy" for another individual found its beginnings within the charismatic movement and simply suggests that one individual could be prayed for on behalf of another while the prayer is shot through his/her body into the person they are "in proxy" for. Truthfully, this belief is New Age in nature and is not found anywhere in the Bible.

The "standing in proxy" idea can be found no place in the Word of God and instead maintains an element of Eastern religion. Often times we have been asked to pray for someone who is "standing in proxy" for another individual. We simply assure them that instead of having them "stand in proxy," we will agree with them in prayer for that person to receive their healing, which is a biblical, godly method of praying for the sick.

QUESTIONS PRIOR TO HEALING PRAYER

There are certain patterns and methods to prayer that can often yield better and quicker results. Here are some practical habits to exercise prior to praying for someone to receive healing:

- Give them good instruction BEFORE you "slap" hands on them. If they are not used to having hands laid upon them they will not understand and may become afraid and uneasy about the situation. By briefly explaining to them what you are doing, you may quickly ease any uncertainty.

- Before you pray with the individual who is sick, ask them what is wrong with them or what part of their body hurts. This should be a brief question, as well as a brief answer. Remember you don't need a 20-minute rundown of all their aches and pains.

- Assure them that miracles are easy, not hard. Assure them that God loves them more than they are able to imagine and He wants them healed even more than they want to be healed.

- It is easy to turn to fear when faced with negative doctor reports, so before you begin to pray for that person respond to them in a positive manner by saying something like, "Everything is easy for Jesus!" This will help rid their mind from fear and move their mind into a place of belief and faith — the good news.

- Build-up their faith by giving them the Word of God. Always remind them that it is God's will for them to be healed.

- Recite for them a testimony of someone who has recently received healing in order to prove to them the reality of the power of God.

- When you pray for the sick speak with authority and boldness. This doesn't require you to shout or scream. Instead be gentle, calm, soothing, and full of boldness. Ask them to look you in the eyes as you heal them. Remember that little, wimpy prayers yield little, wimpy results. Pray with confident boldness just as Jesus did throughout his ministry.

- Keep it brief. Avoid praying long, complicated prayers. Be brief, but powerful. Jesus ministered healing with very few words, *"Be healed,"* or *"stretch out your hand."*

- When you have laid hands on the individual and you have finished praying for them, ask them, "Is it completely gone or a little better?" This will help to show them how quickly God has come to their rescue and is already at work in their body bringing relief and cure.

- Remember that faith is action. Instruct them to do something that they were unable to do before prayer. For example, ask them to move their leg if they were unable to move it previously. Ask them to try and find the pain. Many times they will admit right away that the pain is either completely gone or mostly gone. If it is not completely gone, pray once more. Jesus prayed for the blind man twice before his sight was completely restored.

- Keep in mind that you are not a doctor, and therefore you do not practice medicine. Never encourage someone to throw away medication, prescription glasses, etc. Like it or not, this will come back and negatively affect your ministry.

- Encourage them to revisit their doctor to verify the healing, if necessary. Jesus often times encouraged the sick to return to the temple to verify the healing and lack of sickness or disease.

- Be sensitive to the individual, but most importantly be sensitive to the Holy Spirit and listen for His promptings. If you sense (or know) that the individual is unsaved then lead them to Jesus. This can be done prior to prayer for healing for afterwards. God brought them to you not just to receive healing, but for complete salvation, spirit, soul and body.

Authority of the Believer

"Behold, I give you the authority to trample on serpents and scorpions, and over all the power of the enemy, and nothing shall by any means hurt you." (Luke 10:19 NKJV)

WHAT IS SPIRITUAL AUTHORITY?

Spiritual authority is delegated power. It is divine power, which is bestowed, for the purpose to rule over wickedness, establish righteousness, and dispense justice.

A police officer is a keeper or enforcer of our natural earthly laws. As a police officer he or she is given certain authorities, such as the authority to stop a vehicle on the roadway by merely flashing lights, standing there, and/or holding up his hand. Does that law officer have enough physical power to stop a three-ton vehicle by lifting his hand? The answer is obvious; the officer does not have the physical power to stop the vehicle, yet the individual manning the vehicle recognizes the authority and knows that he must follow instructions. That authority does not come from him, it comes from or is delegated to him from another source and it is given to him in order to effectively do his job. Similarly, the Christian believer has been given authority to effectively do the job. It is our job to heal the sick, mend the broken-hearted, restore sight to the blind, and set the captives free.

*"And Jesus came and spoke to them, saying, 'All **authority** has been given to Me in heaven and on earth...'"* (Matthew 28:18-19 NKJV)

*"And the devil said to Him, "All this **authority** I will give You, and their glory; for this has been delivered to me, and I give it to whomever I wish."* (Luke 4:6)

"...and raised us up together, and made us sit together in the heavenly places in Christ Jesus." (Ephesians 2:6 NKJV)

"You are of God, children, and have overcome them, because He who is in you is greater than he who is in the world." (1 John 4:4 NKJV)

Christ is alive on the inside of every Christian believer. As He is alive with authority and power, so too are we. Jesus is the head of the church and we are His Church, therefore, we function with the same purpose using the same pattern of boldness and authority.

As born again, Spirit-filled believers we must recognize the power and authority that we have been given before we are able to exercise it in our daily life. The reason many believers are bound by fear, sickness, torment, and simple unbelief, is that they have not yet come to the revelation that the very same Spirit that raised Christ from the dead is living and dwelling within them. Stop and take a moment to meditate on the power and authority that it took to raise Christ from the dead. Now meditate on the fact that the very same power and authority was given to you by Jesus and that you have been raised up together with Him, seated next to Him in heavenly places now, in this world, not just the world to come.

*"Most assuredly, I say to you, he who believes in Me, the works that I do he will do also; and **greater works** than these he will do, because I go to My Father. And whatever you ask in My name, that I will do, that the Father may be glorified in the Son. If you ask anything in My name, I will do it."* (John 14:12-14 NKJV)

"...believe the works, that you may know and believe that the Father is in Me, and I in Him." (John 10:38b)

"I and My Father are one." (John 10:30)

"...that they all may be one, as You, Father, are in Me, and I in You; that they also may be one in Us, that the world may believe that You sent Me. And the glory which You gave Me I have given them, that they may be one just as We are one: I in them, and You in Me; that they may be made perfect in one, and that the world may know that You have sent Me, and have loved them as You have loved Me."
(John 17:21-23)

We are one with the Father when we are living a life of Christ. Our God is not weak, powerless, or lame. No. Our God who masterfully created the heavens and the Earth by the power of His Word, whose very breath gives life to all things, the God who, having all power, lowered Himself to be a man, in order that He might fulfill His promise made with the very creation He fashioned. It is time for the Church to wake up and become all that God created us to be.

AUTHORITY, NOT ABUSE

It's true that this teaching has been wickedly twisted and abuse within the Church is the result. Like all scripture, it is meant to help and equip believers, but it can also be perverted and spiritual unhealthiness.

We have been given this authority to reign over the devil and over evil works. We have not been given this authority to rule over other believers. Twisting and perverting the authority of God is witchcraft when it begins to play in the manipulation of the will and emotions of others in order to get them to do what we want.

"I, therefore, the prisoner of the Lord, beseech you to walk worthy of the calling with which you were called, with all lowliness and gentleness, with longsuffering, bearing with

one another in love, endeavoring to keep the unity of the Spirit in the bond of peace. There is one body and one Spirit, just as you were called in one hope of your calling; one Lord, one faith, one baptism; one God and Father of all, who is above all, and through all, and in you all." (Ephesians 4:1-5)

As the body of Christ, we have been given authority in our families, in our personal lives, in our places of employment, in our local church, and to whatever calling that God predestined for us before we were yet born. God called us to DO. God called us to be DOERS. Therefore, we must be responsible with the authority that has been entrusted to us. The place and position of authority should give no place to the devil, allowing him to have no room in any aspect of our earthly lives.

BEING CONSCIENCE OF CHRIST ALONE

"For I resolved to know nothing (to be acquainted with nothing, to make a display of the knowledge of nothing, and to be conscious of nothing) among you except Jesus Christ (the Messiah) and Him crucified." (I Corinthians 2:2)

Throughout our many years of ministry experience, we have witnessed believers give room to the devil by ignorantly giving praise to him. The Word of God and the ministry of Jesus doesn't teach us to acknowledge him, but it instructs us to resist him and overcome him.

Christians can allow the devil into their prayers and without realizing it they pray to him instead of to our Heavenly Father. The same is true with some praise songs that have you singing to the devil. We sing to him, "Get under my feet." Why are we mentioning him at all during a time that should be consecrated to God? Our prayers can be busied with shouts to the devil and acknowledging all that bad that he done. This is a true sign to us that the believer does not have a clear revelation of the authority which lays dormant within them.

In our ministry, we have a policy that never will the devil be mentioned in our singing. The devil doesn't need to be reminded of his defeat during our offering of worship to God. We believe and function out of the knowledge that the devil was already defeated and that he has been made powerless. He is not waiting to be made powerless – he IS powerless now and we will not have him mentioned before God because we desire to only be conscience of and focused on JESUS alone.

Ministry to the Demonized
and Overcoming Demons

DEMONIZATION

To be demonized means to be influenced or under the influence of a demon or demons.

Is it possible for someone who is born again to have a demon? The real question is, "can a demon have a Christian?"

In Dr. Lester Sumrall's book, *Alien Entities*, he tells the story of a woman who was a demoniac. People tried by natural means to get her set free from this wicked control. What they had failed to understand is that the demonic control over the woman was a spiritual problem and therefore, could not be solved by physical or natural means, but rather only by spiritual means.

NO MORE FIGHTING THE DEVIL

One of the largest misconceptions of getting someone free from the devil is that it is a difficult, drawn-out process that requires a real spiritual person who has been fasting for a month. This is just not true. There are times when fasting is necessary for breakthrough, but it is not our job to defeat the devil — he was already defeated through the cross.

*"After this, **Jesus, knowing that all things were now accomplished**, that the Scripture might be fulfilled, said, "I thirst!" Now a vessel full of sour wine was sitting there; and they filled a sponge with sour wine, put it on hyssop, and put*

it *to His mouth. So when Jesus had received the sour wine, He said, "**It is finished!**" And bowing His head, He gave up His spirit. "* (John 19:28)

The blood of Jesus is strong enough to cover EVERY manner of sickness, including mental torment and demonic influence. Much like the time following a war. Once the war is won, the land, riches, and people, are taken by the victor. The war for supernatural control was already won. Jesus was victorious. Now, to the victor goes the spoils.

The devil and all his power has been defeated and rendered powerless. We have already been translated into the heavenly places in Christ Jesus, where with Him we rule and reign.

OUR AUTHORITY OVER DEMONS

"For God did not give us a spirit of timidity, but a spirit of power, of love and of self-discipline. " (I Timothy 1:7 NIV)

"Then they went into Capernaum, and immediately on the Sabbath He entered the synagogue and taught. And they were astonished at His teaching, for He taught them as one having authority, and not as the scribes. Now there was a man in their synagogue with an unclean spirit. And he cried out, saying, "Let us alone! What have we to do with You, Jesus of Nazareth? Did You come to destroy us? I know who You are - the Holy One of God!" But Jesus rebuked him, saying, "Be quiet, and come out of him!" And when the unclean spirit had convulsed him and cried out with a loud voice, he came out of him. Then they were all amazed, so that they questioned among themselves, saying, "What is this? What new doctrine is this? For with authority He commands even the unclean spirits, and they obey Him." And immediately His fame spread throughout all the region around Galilee. " (Mark 1:21-28 NKJV)

With a revelation of the power and authority which is in us, we are able to follow the pattern of how Jesus dealt with demonic confrontations. Jesus did every work with power and authority. He understood His purpose, and he understood His objective. And so must every Christian believer.

- Jesus never carried on or encouraged conversation, of any kind, with any demon. He didn't find it necessary to spend hours talking to devils in order to get someone set free. He simply took authority over them and cast them out. No counseling necessary – only freedom to the captive.

- Jesus always quickly spoke the Word and those who were bound were immediately set free.

- Jesus did not place an emphasis on their presence. When the demon would manifest it was always in an effort to distract from the ministry of truth and life coming from the Master. Jesus was aware of their intention and motivation and would then quickly confront them before continuing on with the ministry work at hand.

DEMONIC DARK PLACES

"...who had his dwelling among the tombs; and no one could bind him, not even with chains, because he had often been bound with shackles and chains. And the chains had been pulled apart by him, and the shackles broken in pieces; neither could anyone tame him." (Mark 5:3-5 NKJV)

People who are under the influence of demons are living in a place of death, just like the demoniac in Mark 5. Those that are influenced by demonic control are strangely attracted to abnormal traits, desires, acts, and other wickedness. In extreme cases of demonic control, such as with serial murderers like John Wayne Gacy, Charles Manson, Jeffery Dahmer, Son of Sam, they all admit that a particular voice spoke to them and told them to commit the heinous murders. They are living in a place of death.

There are different kinds of demonic strongholds that grip people. And most people who struggle with this have somehow learned to "deal with" the condition, often times medicating their body in an effort to coexist. Many, to their detriment, do not understand these things to be of the demonic realm. Following is a list of some of the infirmities, sicknesses, and bondages that come directly from demonic influence:

- Fear and phobias (Closter phobia, arachnophobia, etc.)
- Anxiety attacks (panic attacks)
- Worry, dread, or excessive stress or nervousness
- Suicidal thoughts
- Lusts and fantasies
- Violent anger

As children of the Almighty God we do not "deal with" such oppressive bondage. But how do we overcome? James 4:7 and I Peter 5:6-9 provide the answers.

"Therefore submit to God. Resist the devil and he will flee from you." (James 4:7 NKJV)

"Therefore humble yourselves under the mighty hand of God, that He may exalt you in due time, casting all your care upon Him, for He cares for you. Be sober, be vigilant; because your adversary the devil walks about like a roaring lion, seeking whom he may devour. Resist him, steadfast in the faith, knowing that the same sufferings are experienced by your brotherhood in the world." (Peter 5:6-9 NKJV)

1. Submit your life (thoughts, activities, and desires) to God

2. Cast your cares upon Him knowing that He cares for you

3. Avoid foolishness

4. Be watchful and vigilant over the areas in your life that are not yet as strong as they must become

5. Continually resist the devil. We resist him by occupying our thoughts, time and activities with the things of the Spirit of

God and we resist him by placing our faith in the name, power, and authority of Jesus Christ, our brother, the first Son of the Living God.

My friend, the life of authority is yours for today. The time has come and the authority is for all, not just for some. The glory is upon you in this hour and He has clothed you with Holy Ghost power to GO and to DO and to DELIVER all who are sick and oppressed of the devil. YOU CAN DO IT!

THE AUTHORITY IS YOURS – NOW TAKE IT

We do not need to pray for the devil to be defeated in someone's life, IT IS FINISHED. For lack of knowledge and understanding, many Christians try to counsel the devil instead to cast him out or to expel him. Others mistake authority to be the same as screaming, begging, or pleading.

Authority is the key word when dealing with devils and demons. As Christians, we have God-given authority in the name of Jesus. Devils only obey authority. Authority comes from confidence — confidence in the position you hold with your Father. Like Father, like son. And authority comes from your confidence in the finished work of the cross. Jesus did it all, now you get it all.

We are able to learn a great amount about how to deal with devils and demons from the ministry of Jesus. Jesus used His authority and rather than talking to the devil or demon, He cast it out. Having no fear and using his voice, He commanded that they leave and be cast out.

Churches have been prophesying to each other for years. They've been hoping, fasting, and casting down spirits for decades, all to no affect. Often times the Church misses revival because it fails to realize that it doesn't require spiritual mapping or spiritual warfare sessions in order to live. Phillip didn't need to go down to the local library and find out who was murdered and cast out that spirit and do spiritual warfare in order to have the Samaritan revival. The same is true in our lives and in the local church.

Remember, they are powerless. Take authority. Cast them out.

Ministering in Power

*"And with **great** power the apostles gave witness to the resurrection of the Lord Jesus. And **great** grace was upon them all."* (Acts 4:33)

IMPACT BEFORE OUTFLOW

The early church received the baptism of the Holy Spirit and when that took place there was a powerful flow of the glory of God that was transferred into their very being. It was miracle-working power that burned through them and it was the love of Christ that motivated their works for the Kingdom.

The time between Acts 2 and the persecution of the Christians in Acts 4 is not a long period. We know that up until that time the influence of the early churches witness of the passion of the Christ and of the power of God was vast and wide-reaching. In Acts 4:33, Luke says, *"...with **great** power...and **great** grace was upon them all."* The Greek word for "great" is *Mega*. So, more appropriately, it should read, *"... and with **mega** power... and **mega** grace was upon them all."* They were continually receiving mega grace outpourings and they were continually at work giving it away.

In 1997, we first heard of the thundering revival at the Toronto Blessing. We heard the negatives of course, but we also heard about the glorious outpouring of God's love and great grace that was upon the people. Not long after we initially learned about what God was doing among the believer's there, we decided to visit Toronto Airport Christian Fellowship where the revival was hosted.

The worship was wonderful and so very deep and powerful. Thousands were present and together, as one, we sung with great fervency and passion about our love for God. We noticed people from every Christian religious background that you could imagine. There were Catholics, Lutherans, Anglicans, Pentecostals and of course, Charismatics. That particular night there were several Catholic nuns and priests on their knees weeping, laughing and shaking under the presence of God's goodness. Later, Pastor John Arnott preached a message that was timely and pointed and it pierced our hearts. People were moved to tears as he skillfully and surgically aimed at the people's inner-man, our spirit, with his words.

As it came time for prayer ministry, we made our way to the designated area to receive. I was hungry for an impartation of the flow of tender love and grace that I had found in this place. The "prophetic teams" began to pray for everyone in the building. I waited patiently for a team to come to me.

I had been preparing for my first ministry trip to Norway, which was less than two weeks away. And although I was preparing to go, I really hadn't been thinking at all that night about my trip.

A couple gracefully walked up to me to pray for me and just as they were to begin they stopped and pointed to my shoes, then my pants, and then the shirt I was wearing. He said, *"Sometimes the exterior reveals the interior. I can see that you will soon be going to over the ocean to take the blood of Jesus and it will bring holiness to a people that you've never seen before."* That night, I was wearing a new pair of bright white tennis shoes, blue jeans and a bright red shirt. Each color was a representation of what was to come. God used this seemingly silly analogy to reach me with His power. I fell to the carpet with a thud as God confirmed to me that I was on the right path in my ministry pursuits. There was such an impartation and infilling within me of God's power that night, and I didn't realize how great it was until I arrived to minister in Norway, just ten days later.

I tell you this story because it is important that we as believers and ministers of God's power learn how to minister out of an overflow. When God fills us to overflowing it is that overflowing that must be given away. The power is found in the overflow, the anointing of God is found in the overflow, and the hungry ones are fed from the overflow. The overflow is the greater "mega" Spirit upon us, and with it the greater "mega" power and grace will flow through us to others.

SAY GOODBYE TO THE FEAR OF MAN

Many people would admit that they are afraid of something. Some have fears of animals, snakes, heights, water, large spaces, small spaces, etc. More people are stricken with the fear of man than all of the other fears of the world combined. *"The fear of man brings a snare,"* it says in Proverbs and surely the fear of man has "caught" many in its web, paralyzing them with its squeezing force. We believe that the fear of man is the number one reason why most Christians do not evangelize and witness.

The greatest lesson that the Holy Spirit ever taught us about fear is that we, Christians, must rebel against fear until it no longer rules over our mind. The only way to break the spirit of fear is to rebel against it with everything within you. To rebel against it we must move in the opposite spirit. If fear says, "Don't ask her if you can pray for her. She looks like she would be mean and reject you," then DO IT. Walk boldly up to her and ask her if she'd allow you to pray for her. Do whatever fear tells you not to do. That is godly rebellion and every Christian should walk in it.

"For God has not given us a spirit of fear, but of power and of love and of a sound mind." (2 Timothy 1:7)

We were home and off the road for a couple days when Susie and I decided to go to the gym for a quick workout. As we were driving to the gym I told the Lord that I really wanted Him to use me to heal the sick that day. As we walked into the doors I scanned our membership card when we overheard one of the employees, a young lady, and her manager. We arrived mid-conversation, but we heard the manager say to the young lady, "Yeah, I really need to start going to church again. I haven't been to church in over 10 years." The young lady shook her head in agreement and told him that she too hadn't been to church in about five years. Overhearing their conversation was an obvious Holy Spirit set-up and we knew that God was about to use us to do something powerful to demonstrate His love to them.

It was time for me to walk on water. I said to the manager, Chris, "I am so glad to have overheard your conversation. I am a man of God, a minister. They were shocked. I went on, "When I saw you, God told me that you have pain in your left shoulder. That is true, isn't it?" Chris shook his head. I said, "I sense that God sent us here to minister to you to SHOW you that God wants a relationship with you." My words just hung there in the air as Chris's eyes got big. He confirmed that he had a terrible injury while training in the martial arts, and his left rotator cuff was damaged. I asked him if I could please pray for him and see what happens. He nodded his head again and we began to pray a very simple prayer. *"God, you brought us here at this moment on this day to bring Chris the message that You love him and that You care about him. So, we now command healing to come into his shoulder. Thank you Jesus."* With that prayer the presence of God was instantly there, thick and tangible. Chris smiled and said that the pain had instantly left his shoulder. With great joy He raised his arm for the first time in over a year. Right there in the gym doorway, Chris bowed his head and thanked Jesus asking to receive Him and to be filled with the same Holy Spirit power.

We were rebelling against the voice of fear that morning. We both felt that initial grip of fear as we interrupted their conversation. But in our hunger to manifest Christ on earth we stepped out there and ministered with boldness and look what God did.

"Practice evangelism until evangelism becomes your practice."
– Brian Blount, *From the Sanctuary to the Streets*

POWER UP AND BE BOLD

We must set ourselves up for ministering to the lost in power. There are practical things that we can do to power ourselves up and walk out in boldness. Jesus gave us a clue to one of those practical tools in Mark 6.

*"And He called the twelve to Himself, and began to send them out **two by two**, and gave them power over unclean spirits."* (Mark 6:7 NKJV)

Pairing or teaming up with at least one other person is a great way to power evangelize. As partners in ministry you can rely on each other to keep aware of others around you who may be in need of ministry. It is also a great tool for accountability and going with someone will help to empower you both for greater ministry opportunities, while encouraging each other to rebel against fear. Remember Peter in Acts 3? The Bible says that Peter had his friend, John, with him and that they boldly ministered to the lame man at the city gate.

*"As **iron sharpens iron**, so a man sharpens the countenance of his friend."* (Proverbs 27:17)

*"Now, Lord, look on their threats, and grant to Your servants that with all **boldness** they may speak Your word, by stretching out Your hand to heal, and that signs and wonders may be done through the name of Your holy Servant Jesus. ...and they spoke the word of God with **boldness**."* (Acts 4:29-31)

Go Ahead, Show Off Your Power

"Or what woman, having ten silver coins, if she loses one coin, does not light a lamp, sweep the house, and search carefully until she finds it? And when she has found it, she calls her friends and neighbors together, saying, 'Rejoice with me, for I have found the piece which I lost!' Likewise, I say to you, there is joy in the presence of the angels of God over one sinner who repents." (Luke 15:8-10)

POWER EVANGELISM

Power evangelism is evangelism outreach that is driven by the supernatural power of God to set people free using signs, wonders, miracles and the prophetic.

The Church doesn't have a shortage of ways and means to evangelize the world for Jesus. Some use tracts and others use a script to evangelize. Any and every method of evangelism is good and are great ways to motivate people to reach out to the lost. There is one method that stands out above the rest. This is the most commonly used method of the New Testament and it has a very long lasting effect of salvation in greater measure. This method is called, power evangelism. When power evangelism is ministered to the lost there is such a deep and impacting touch of the Holy Spirit that the person has to realize that he or she desires a continual relationship with God.

There are many ways of being used in power evangelism. The term "power evangelism" was coined by Pastor John Wimber in his book, *Power Evangelism*. It was a best-selling book, but has been out of print for decades. Pastor John Wimber attributed the success of revival and growth of his church to power evangelism. His small church grew from 200 members to several thousand members in just a years time because the people were moving in power on the streets of their city.

Power evangelism is simply performing miracles, healing the sick, giving prophetic words, etc. outside of the church in order to impact the lost with a presentation of the powerful Gospel of Christ.

Below are a few methods of power evangelism that you should use to minister to the lost, in power, wherever you may be.

- Facebook evangelism (prophetic words, getting names, pictures, etc.)
- Highlight evangelism (who is God showing you to minister to)
- Look for the sick – those who are in obvious need for healing
- Treasure Hunts – Ask God for "spiritual clues" as to whom to minister, what do they look like, what is their name, where you will find them, and what does that person need?
- New Age or psychic fairs
- Dream interpretation or prophetic words booth at local coffee shops or popular areas
- Dream Interpretation
- Go to the local Mall with the purpose of healing the sick
- Emergency Room ministry to the sick

Here are some ways to increase the hunger and passion for the miraculous to move in your daily life.

- **Desire Spiritual Gifts** — as the scripture teaches us, we must desire it before it occurs in our lives. If you don't desire it, you'll never pursue it, and if you don't pursue it, you'll not have it. Everything in the Kingdom of God begins and continues with your desire.

- **Impartation** — Ask others who are already doing the miraculous to lay hands on you and pray for a transferring or an impartation. When you see someone being used in a particular method of the Kingdom of God, go and ask him or her to lay hands on you for an impartation of the anointing on their life.

- **Go for it!** — Just go and step out in faith. Jump into the water and begin to do the stuff! We cannot learn everything just by reading. We must also learn by doing.

- **Open Your Heart to the Lost** — be compassionate toward people and be sympathetic to their circumstance, pains, and weaknesses.

- **Be Willing to Fail or Be Rejected** — Don't take it personal when people reject you or ridicule you in your attempt to minister life to them. Be willing to fail and make mistakes. We always remind our team members that it is alright to fail, but it is never alright to give up.

- **Test It Out** — Ask those to whom you minister if they feel better after your prayers. Do they feel "heat" or tingling in their body? Healing can often times take place, but they may not realize that they are getting better as God's working on them if you don't ask.

What else can you do to cultivate a supernatural evangelism mindset? Here are a few things that will really inspire your faith and equip you for Kingdom ministry.

1. Read books/listen to messages on the subject of supernatural ministry.

2. Start to pray for divine appointments and power encounters to minister to the lost.

3. Go through your New Testament and study the times of supernatural ministry. Learn what key things were done in those different settings and situations.

4. Start to "experiment/try" ministering to people in public in power.

(You may download free evangelism materials from our website at: www.SHAREtheFIRE.org)

Recommended Reading

- *Power Evangelism* – John Wimber
- *Power Healing* – John Wimber
- *From the Sanctuary to the Streets* – Brian Blount
- *Supernatural Power of a Renewed Mind* – Bill Johnson
- *Ultimate Treasure Hunt* – Kevin Dedmon

About the Authors

Tom & Susie Scarrella

Tom Scarrella is the founder/president of *Scarrella Ministries*, an international traveling ministry based out of Fort Lauderdale, Florida. Tom is also the founder and director of *Ministry Training Institute* (MTI), a correspondence based ministry training program. In addition, Tom and his wife, Susie, host and produce their own weekly television program, *"All for the Kingdom,"* which airs in over 200 million homes around the globe.

At the HEART of *Scarrella Ministries*, revival burns. It is their passion to see the body of Jesus Christ fervently set ablaze with Grace, Truth, Miracles, and with the Power of God, reaching out to a lost world to establish the Kingdom of God among men.

Beginning in the ministry in 1986, Tom pastored until 1994 when after transitioning their entire ministry, he founded *Scarrella Ministries* and began traveling worldwide igniting revival fires. Since their marriage in 2003, together Tom and Susie, have ministered in over twenty nations and in every one of the United States of America.

Since their ministry's inception, they have continued to minister with a strong emphasis on *Revival, Passion, and the Power of God*. As a ministry, since 2003 they have been witness to a mighty increase in miracles, signs, and wonders as unlike any other time in the history of Scarrella Ministries. As a result, thousands have been healed from blindness, deafness, lameness, and diseases. And just as with the commission of the early disciples, SIGNS and WONDERS follow their ministry.

"And my speech and my preaching was not with enticing words of man's wisdom, but in demonstration of the Spirit and of power: That your faith should not stand in the wisdom of men, but in the power of God."

\- I Corinthians 2:4-5

Tom Scarrella Ministries
www.SHAREtheFIRE.org
phone 954-336-5993

WWW.SHARETheFIRE.ORG

GUARANTEED
TO CAUSE YOUR YOUTH GROUP TO GROW BY MORE THAN 100% IN JUST 10 WEEKS!

Ministry Training Institute
shaping students into LEADERS

revival
passion
zeal
creativity
purpose
servanthood
practical ministry training
discipleship

An inexpensive correspondence bible school
for all ministry minded individuals

www.ministrytraininginstitute.com

Made in the USA
Charleston, SC
26 February 2014